The Myth of

"ME"

A handbook to assist us toward sanity

Tony Spatarella

The Myth of "ME"
 A handbook to assist us toward sanity

Published by CaryPress

www.CaryPress.com

Printed in the United States of America

CONTENTS

Preface

Preface

This handbook was conceived and created for the purpose of investigation. The focus of the investigation is on the sense of self that is so near and dear to us, and yet, so problematic….the focus is on "ME"….

The majority of individuals on this planet are not paying attention. So much of what is thought, said, and done comes from a programmed response, a tendency to react to situations without full awareness. Hiding in the shadows is an imaginary self-image that more often than not runs our lives. We call this seemingly solid and permanent sense of self, "ME"….

"ME" develops as a result of a state of confusion regarding who we truly are, and who we truly are not. Most human beings are plagued with this identity crisis that causes a feeling of discontent, which manifests as afflictive thoughts and emotions….

When we begin the inquiry process regarding the true nature of our being, many discoveries will take place. We will become aware of the many aspects of our personality that are completely conditioned by external events. We will begin to see lies everywhere, and we will realize that "ME" is at the center of this deception. It is the central lie that distorts our perceptions and creates a state of anxiety and confusion.

This book may be very helpful in making you look at your inner reality, your experience of "ME", with discernment and clarity...Contemplate the words... Engage the practices, and most of all, pay attention!

There are infinite possibilities of perception and expression beyond the prison walls of the imaginary sense of self, called "ME". Enter into this journey with an open mind and heart; The truth is waiting to be discovered, behind the veil of the person you think you are....Behind the veil of "ME"...

Tony Spatarella
2014

1 CHAPTER - JUST WHAT EXACTLY IS "ME"?

The center of your universe is "ME"....

It is your name, your story, your associations, your ideas, your beliefs, your memories, your self-image, your very identity. "ME" is who you 'think' you are.....

It is not your body, because if I ask you whose body that is as I point to you, you will say it's mine, it belongs to "ME". So, the body is merely a possession of "ME", not "ME" itself.

It appears that "ME" wants to be happy but it rarely is, and when it is, that won't be the case for too long.

"ME" feels separate from the world. It looks out upon the world, dividing it into things that benefit "ME", and things that don't. The world can be very threatening to "ME" and usually is.

Emotions happen to "ME". When you feel that you are happy, sad, fearful, joyful, angry, loving, jealous, envious, etc., all of these happen to "ME"….

Look closely. "ME" wants, and wants, and wants almost constantly, and is never truly satisfied.

"ME" wants to live forever. That is it's only true goal….continuity. It wants to secure a happy future but forever dwells in unhappiness trying to get there.

"ME" requires an eternal heaven somewhere in the future, or endless reincarnations to feel secure, but "ME" knows that these ideas are not provable, so "ME" creates beliefs, faith, and endless theories to make it feel better. That tactic works to some degree, but "ME" is never really sure, and that is the reason that hope and faith are required. "ME" hopes for a happy ending that will never come, and

"ME" knows this all too well deep down. That is why "ME" can never truly be happy. "ME" is the main ingredient in unhappiness, anxiety, and misery. Why is "ME" so miserable, so often?

Can I fix "ME"? We are always trying to but that only tends to bring us more stress and pain. We can't fix it because "ME" itself is the problem; It's a disease of the mind, and it isn't real...

It isn't real, but it's all we know and so we cling to "ME" as if it were reality itself, the only reality.

The unknown is not particularly inviting, so this bundle of memories, beliefs and identifications we call "ME", becomes our safe haven, even if it is never fully at peace, even if it is the source of misery and fear.

"I" is not "ME". When we say "I", there is some truth to it. "I" is much more fluid than "ME". "I" lives in the present moment, at least some of the time. "I" am thinking, "I" am walking, "I" am eating.... it is possible for "I" to speak the truth. "ME" clings to the past and fears the future. It is a manufactured self-image and it is always false, always a lie...

9

Of course, when you have "ME", you have 'MINE'. All possessive thoughts, feelings and actions, come from "ME". My body, my money, my job, my car, my wife, my husband, my child, my family, my religion, my nation….it goes on and on. "ME" is always building its territory, always trying to prove itself. The goal, it tells itself, is that it wants to be happy, to be fulfilled; that is one of the lies. "ME" just wants to continue, even if it is usually miserable; any identity will do. This misery comes from "ME" trying to maintain itself. "ME" is trying to hold itself together as a solid, permanent entity in a world of movement; constant flux and change. This is why "ME" can never be fully at peace and often exists in a state of frustration, anger, fear, or sadness...

"ME" feels unworthy……. it can never live up to what it imagines it can be, and it knows this to be true. Deep down, it knows that it isn't real, so it looks the other way. All distractions serve "ME" in its quest for continuity. Television, movies, sporting events, concerts, video games, surfing the net; all of it, while not inherently destructive, serves to keep "ME" amused; distracted just enough to not look at what is really going on; at what is really there...or isn't there....

There are philosophies and spiritual teachings that refer frequently to "ME"; It has many names. Ego, suffering self, pain body, false self, ignorance, delusion….. it is the source of suffering. It is not really you; STOP believing it!

There may truly be a heaven, or reincarnation of souls evolving, but "ME" has no real interest in these things. "ME" enjoys looking into the future, striving for a heavenly reward, dreaming about its future lives. It pretends to want heaven, but fears the idea of leaving its comfy abode, its little narrow box. "ME" wants to stay right where it is, looking ahead for the sake of looking ahead. It shuns heaven and creates its own private hell….

"ME" is not always in charge, and that is the good news. Have you noticed times when you have felt peaceful and connected to the world? These moments may be rare for some and more frequent for others, but they are a true peek behind the veil of "ME". There is something much greater than "ME" trying to get your attention. The truth is calling out for you to see the lie you have been living. The days of being "ME" are numbered……

To go beyond the lie of "ME", you will first have to understand how "ME" is created and what supports it. This knowledge will give you the possibility of dissolving "ME" and living a connected, authentic life.

2 CHAPTER - CREATING "ME"

P art of the explanation of how "ME" is created

and sustains itself can involve the idea of past lives; reincarnation. I will not dwell on that during the course of this book, but it is important to address it to some degree, just in case there is truth to the process of birth, death, and rebirth.

If reincarnation is true, then what we became in past lives through our conditioning and experiences will carry over into this one. Tendencies, habits, predispositions... Memories that exist in the subconscious mind of the individual can be triggered in this life and "ME" will then react from a habit pattern, which involves the thought process and emotions. Further reactions will reinforce the habit energy and "ME" will be up to its old tricks.

The idea of reincarnation can explain how the individual is already wired to behave and react in certain programmed patterns, but it is not necessary to dwell on past lives to understand how "ME" is created. It is an ongoing process, so from this point on, we will explore how "ME" develops in this life, keeping in mind that it is possibly supported by 'past' existences.

A baby is born into this world....no "ME", not yet anyway. Since "ME" is a mind created sense of self, the infant has no opportunity to create "ME" because its mind is not sufficiently developed at this point in time.

As the child grows, it begins to interact, to play, to walk, and to explore its environment. The parents, who both have "ME" fully activated, begin to teach the child to be a "ME". "No, don't touch that", "Be a good boy", "You are a bad girl", "This is good", "That is bad", and so on. The parents are now in the process of creating a "ME"....a 'person'......

The conditioning process has begun, and the child is slowly constructing a self-image. The child is being told what it is by its well-intentioned parents who have their own personal biases and interpretations of reality; their own fully-functioning "ME"......

Relatives, friends, and other children will also contribute to this creation of "ME" as the child continues to experience the world and remembers these experiences, which have formed thought patterns energized by emotions.

"ME" is developing quickly, then comes school, new friends, television, movies...."ME" is growing and growing. It is being completely molded by external circumstances and the child takes for granted that what it is being told about itself and the world is true; It isn't, but it is never questioned, because all of the mad scientists that are contributing to creating this new "ME" have never questioned what they have been told.

"ME" can only exist in unconsciousness. It requires a lack of awareness and insight. "ME" is taken for granted and is accepted as true. The child would never dream that it is surrounded by lies, but the painful truth is that there are lies everywhere. Hardly anyone is questioning their existence, trying to understand this life, this world, this state of being….

As "ME" moves into adolescence, the conditioning continues, with a sprinkle of hormones on top for good measure. This is a very challenging time for "ME" as the external environment becomes more influential than ever. "ME" seeks acceptance and connection in a world that seems less stable and more threatening. "ME" is getting more solid; it is trying to know itself amidst relentlessly changing moods and circumstances. It is a hypersensitive "ME" at this point in time, and its identity is now a lot like Jello. Its self-image has solidified much more than during childhood, but it still feels flimsy and unstable.

And then, congratulations "ME"! You have now graduated to adulthood and have further contracted into a solid mass of beliefs, fears, anxiety, and confusion.

"ME" is now attempting to find status in a world of other "ME's" that want to see you fail. It has become a competition for success and happiness, as if you could ever be happy continually engaging in such a stressful endeavor.... The world has gone MAD.....

Under such dire circumstances, "ME" chooses to escape into a thick cloud of distraction. The whole society is wallowing in the media driven amusement machine. All of the "ME's" share the same frustration, so they disappear for a while just to feel some temporary peace; but it doesn't last long enough. Maybe have a drink, or two, or three....maybe take a pill, or go to a strip club, or go shopping....so many places to hide, but all of it is merely a band aid on a gaping, festering wound; that wound is "ME"......

There are levels of intensity of "ME"; at times it can be relatively at peace for a while, only to erupt with afflictive emotional outbursts if one of its buttons has been pushed. Other "ME's" are always or nearly always in a heightened state of suffering due to stress, fear, anger, or sadness. We can also observe individuals that appear to be free of "ME" to a large degree. There are two possible explanations for this non-"ME" manifestation. One possibility is someone who has become such an expert at suppressing "ME" and its pain, that they are unaware on a conscious level of the "ME" that is bubbling and smoldering under the surface. Beware of this hidden "ME"; its' eruption can have catastrophic effects on the environment. We may lament "I can't believe he exploded that way; he was such a nice guy, and so calm"! The other possibility is an individual whose "ME" is shrinking significantly due to an increase of awareness, or the Sage that has become completely free of this insidious, illusory beast. This is a rare individual, but you are potentially the same as that Sage....we all are.....

"ME", it's all about "ME". One of the classic traits of this contraction of mental and emotional energy is its intense focus on itself. "ME" is totally self-absorbed. In extreme cases it can engage in excessive pride and overrate its own worth, or feel completely worthless, and dwell upon that endlessly. Once created, "ME" will continue to reinforce its imaginary existence by creating new thought forms, and emotions that will energize it and keep the illusion alive. It will become you....."ME" has become you. Another cosmic beast is born and lives among us……

Your very identity….

Which is a mind-created fiction….

Is firmly based on the lie of

"ME"….

© Beverlee Horowitz

3 CHAPTER - "ME", THE IDENTITY BUILDER

Who are you? If I ask you that question, you

will tell me a story based on where you came from, what you did, what you do, what you believe, what you like, what you dislike, and so on....

You are a bundle of accumulated experiences placed in a file with your name on it....Judy, John, Torrance, Melinda....all of them have one thing in common; they also call themselves "ME". The other names are merely subtitles in the story of "ME".

Our identities are precious to us, and yet they are a major pain in the ass at the same time. Somehow creating this safe haven also has a downside, if we are willing to see it. We have completely limited ourselves and have become predictable machines in a mechanized world.

Once our mechanistic identities are solid enough, we begin the program of protecting its existence from the other machines that may be trying to destroy us.... irrational fear becomes part of "ME".

We love names and labels; "ME" has many sub-categories that assist in the identity building process. Your birth name, nicknames that are acquired through the years, along with labels that describe things that you do. Teacher, banker, musician, student, mother, father, custodian, criminal, prostitute, politician, and so on and on...

Names and labels are convenient and useful in the world of beings and objects that we are functioning in presently. They are useful in describing aspects of phenomena that we encounter on a daily basis. Often, however, if not always, we go too far and take these labels as absolute reality. We create entities and concepts based on a small amount of data that we collect with our sensory apparatus, which is fed directly to our mental consciousness. This 'mind' immediately puts the new data into a system of categorization that is already wired with its own biases, tendencies, and pre-conceptions......

Over time we build up a conceptual network that labels objects and beings, and we believe the label to be the whole truth. We do it with the world we encounter; most of all, we do it with "ME".

Our identity, which we cling to so tightly, is very unstable, a castle built on sand. The slightest change can trigger a tremendous state of anxiety. "ME" will have to figure out how to reconstruct itself if it loses a spouse, or a job, or an acquired status in society. We so want to keep it together; to keep "ME" intact as a solid dependable focus of attention. Of course we know that at any time things can shift, sometimes dramatically, and "ME" will be exposed as a mere ghost in our mind. That is our greatest fear….that we don't exist….it haunts us. That is why "ME" looks away, at anything else.

"ME" is constructed out of experiences and memories. We believe these events are happening to someone. A being is there collecting the content, putting labels on it, dividing it up into a good pile and a bad pile. The Identity is built up over time and always has a main attribute; a style of being based on the content of experiences.

The identity of "ME", however, is never singular or whole. Even if the identity has a central theme that has been firmly established, for example a very sad and despondent identity, it also has many other characteristics that develop due to the immense amount of data it receives.

The multiple characteristics of "ME" may not always get along. Some may even clash with its main attribute, which is the central identity, the central theme of "ME". This creates more anxiety and confusion. "ME" has become an entity at war with itself and now feels threatened from within and without.

There are times that we intentionally engage in the

process of changing "ME". These are pivotal moments in our life, when we actually seek to change our core identity. Spiritual practitioners may change their name, take vows, and modify their behavior as they become fully immersed in the formalized aspect of their new religion or belief system. The identity shifts, then re-solidifies into a new 'person'; a new "ME".

This identity shifting can become its own game, and creates an illusion of fluidity. This, however, is not the case, as "ME" is always solidifying during this process. It remains in charge, but keeps changing its mask...now I am so and so...my new name is.....The core identity may change, but "ME" continues on, feeling safe and secure as it acts out its new role....

"ME" uses identities as an anchor. Identities for some are solid and predictable throughout a lifetime. For others, identities may come and go, but "ME" always remains in either case. The self-image continues on, and the truth remains hidden, but you are not "ME".... You are the truth.....

You are a great writer of Fiction....

Your masterpiece is

"ME".....

It isn't real.......

There are many factors that influence the construction of an identity; ethnicity is one of those common factors. "ME" usually feels very at home with identification to a particular ethnicity, or race.... I'm Italian, I'm Mexican, I'm Black, and so on....When you identify with a group, your identity is energized by the other group members. This is very reinforcing to "ME", but if you look closely, you will not find anything Italian, or Mexican, or Black about you. Skin color itself tells us nothing. There are light skinned Blacks, and very dark skinned Italians and Mexicans. The molecules and atoms that make up our physical bodies have no ethnicity or race; neither does our blood....

When we look closely at our minds, however, we see how the IDEA of being a particular ethnicity or race manifests in our consciousness. We are conditioned by cultural attitudes and beliefs, and a very strong identity is born in us. This is sustained by the group energy that we are surrounded by; it is in your mind only. Strong identifications like ethnicity and race, keep "ME" fat and happy....

So, culture plays a major role in the process of conditioning and domestication. Instead of being a celebration of diversity and creativity, culture is taken very seriously and has become a major tool in the building of an identity. We are so serious, and we will defend our identities, even violently if we feel threatened enough....

Culture is not only about ethnicity or race. We have what appears to be an infinite number of sub-cultures to belong to; musicians, football players, teachers, actors, bankers.... the list is endless, and we can belong to as many as we choose. All of these sub-cultures are further conditioning factors that have their own sets of values, beliefs, ideas, and activities. They will create more identities within the core identity; the receptacle for this diverse group of identities is "ME". It is the one constant in the tumultuous sea of identities that have been accumulated over time. It is important to remember that these identities are the life blood of "ME". It will use whatever it can to stay intact....

To be a person….To be a "ME"….

"ME" is a danger to your peace of mind, to your emotional state, and to your quality of life. It is also a danger to society, to the world at large. But how can a puny little "ME" affect a society? How can it influence the world? It can't, and so…….

Let me introduce you to what is potentially the most destructive force on the planet…"WE". As we saw with ethnicity, race, and the various sub-cultures, groups have the power to move mountains if they are large enough, and if their belief systems are strong enough. A large group of "ME's" that resonate together for a belief or a cause will assemble and energize into a fully functioning, powerful "WE"…."WE", like "ME" has an agenda. It wants to survive, to grow, to continue. Anything, including other "WE's", will be viewed as a threat to its survival if the beliefs are not compatible; if they are too different…..

The "WE" I am referring to is not a connectedness to our fellow humans as a whole. "WE", like "ME", is a contraction based on a story; in this case a shared story. This "WE" is a limitation, a sub-group of humanity that will defend its point of view, which is its very life source. Religions, nations, ethnic and racial groups, members of a particular 'class' in a society....all of these and many more can and often do, become a "WE" that wants to survive and thrive, often at the expense of anything or anyone that will stand in its way......

All warfare on this planet has emerged due to a "WE" against "WE" conflict. There have been 'Holy Wars'; a Christian "WE" vs. an Islamic "WE". Wars over land ownership; an Israeli "WE" vs. a Palestinian "WE". There has even been in our own nation, which is supposed to be based on the principals of freedom and democracy, a North "WE" vs. a South "WE"....

A planet of insane "ME's" and "WE's" trying to survive, to continue....yet, destroying themselves in the process...Madness!

It doesn't work, but "ME" and "WE" have no reasoning ability, no awareness of anything outside of their own ideology. The story and identity of "ME" and "WE" must continue, get bigger and stronger; it's about survival; about protecting a mind created self-image that has no real existence. It's all a dream that has become a nightmare, and "ME" and "WE" are afraid to wake up!

Fear of the unknown, fear of not being a particular thing among other things; fear of space, of non-existence...."ME and "WE" are just fear, after all....a delusion based on the fear that there is no solid ground, nothing to depend on; nothing to keep us safe and secure. There may be just 'nothing', and "ME" and "WE" are having none of it.....

So, "ME" and "WE" must continue on as a 'something', avoiding at all costs what appears to be a great void...death, non-existence...Attachment to form is the survival mechanism, and "ME" and "WE" are safe, for now....

This feeling of safety and security that "ME" and "WE" foolishly adhere to is a great self-deception. There is no safety in a universe of phenomena that is changing constantly, there is only movement. There are not even any objects moving about in space; the objects themselves ARE movement! No solidity, no stability at all, and yet, "ME" and "WE" go on blindly attempting to grow and thrive, secure in a false identity that is completely make believe.

An identity created by a mind that constructs a phantasmagoria of shadows onto an imaginary screen...."ME" and "WE" are just a movie....a dark comedy in reality; a drama in their own fantasy world....

All identities are masks, a persona....

Look closely at your own core identity and at all of its sub-plots.....Is there anything there that is really true?

The problem of "ME" and "WE" on our planet is creating a dysfunction in our species that could possibly lead toward our destruction. Humanity is in grave danger; our planet may be as well....

Amazingly, all of this insanity is due to the simple mechanism of building a self, a "ME", with our own memories and imaginations. It appears that the will to survive and instinctual fear, which are natural for the preservation of our bodies, has gone haywire in our minds. We try to protect every memory, concept, feeling, and all of the self-images that these produce. We try to prevent them from coming to an end. All of it has become so automatic, so habitual. Humans have become robots whose programs are imbued with confusion and fear....

If "ME" and "WE" would just look at what is really going on, without bias, without fear....but this is not in their nature, and yet, it is possible to look within because YOU are not "ME". You can simply turn the camera lens around and see "ME" objectively. It is possible to see clearly and to be fully aware. Is "ME" ready and willing to do that? No.... are you? It would take a tremendous amount of courage, for sure. "ME" will likely cower in fear at the thought of this, but once it has been pointed out to you that "ME" is nothing but a lie, a mirage, a dream; once you have had this seed planted in your mind, the possibility of freedom and truth will have been realized. "ME" will be completely reluctant to engage in this endeavor, and will probably seek further distraction to make sure that you avoid looking too closely, but there is now a glimmer of light in the darkness....you have already heard and seen too much.....

If you are brave enough...Curious enough.....Then it may be time to engage in the process if dissolving "ME"......

Do it out of love for yourself, out of love for the world...Do it for the love of truth.

© Daniel St. Aubin

4 CHAPTER - DISSOLVING "ME"

There are many circumstances that will lead you to look at "ME" directly, with the intention to be free of its tyranny......

One possibility is to become sick and tired of the stress, anxiety, fear, and limitation that this imaginary beast has somehow imposed upon you. You may be done with the suffering and ready to break out of the icy grip of "ME".

Some will try to end the pain by killing the body, but we can't be sure that some part of the tormented mind won't continue on after the body's demise, having now added on new layers of sorrow and confusion....too risky....another approach is required.......

We are so intelligent; we know that something has to come to an end, but is it the physical form? It may be easy, perhaps, to have the correct agenda, but many will focus on the wrong target. The correct target is the mind created "ME"...

For others, the inspiration to be rid of "ME" may manifest mysteriously, intuitively. Something may just feel not quite right about the quality of this existence. There may be an inner momentum building in the mind that seeks answers regarding the absurdity of this life....

Many will begin to seek answers through the process of understanding the human psyche. Others may begin to read philosophical or spiritual books that focus on the 'ego' as an enemy that must be destroyed, or transcended. There may be these and many other approaches to solving the problem of "ME"….

What these approaches have in common is the realization, first of all, that there is a problem. Life is a struggle, at least more often than we would like it to be. There is not enough joy, or love, or creativity.

This epiphany is a major step toward liberation. If you don't want to acknowledge the problem of "ME", you will continue to hide. In truth, it's "ME" that is doing the hiding and extending your suffering. The world is filled with enough distractions to keep you looking away from the quagmire "ME" has created for an entire lifetime and beyond. Many choose this path until they hit rock bottom, and many die in a state of delusion….you don't have to……Knowledge of the disease will bring you closer to the cure. If you already know too much, and have seen too much, then burying your head in the sand is ludicrous. It is now impossible to turn away. It's time to come face to face with "ME"….

It is important to prepare the ground before embarking on an exploration of "ME" and all of its nuances. The exploration process is essential. You have to know directly what "ME" is and isn't to have any chance of escaping its grasp. The assumption is that "ME" is you, it's who you are. "ME" is the totality of your being. That is what "ME" tells you, but "ME" is a liar.…."ME" is a lie.……

Preparing the ground is a simple process. Really, all of it is simple. It is "ME" that creates layers of complication and confusion. So, to prepare the ground, we will use the breath and the body as our anchor….our support……

Right now, become fully aware of your body.….Be aware especially of your hands and feet….Just feel the body without creating dialogue in your mind….

Feel the energy and life force in the body…Just be one with it for a few minutes….

Once you have established this connection to the body, become aware of your breath as well….Breathe naturally…. Gently watch the breath enter and exit your body.….Do this for a few minutes as well….You may notice that your breathing slows down naturally during this process….Notice anything that comes into your awareness, but refrain from any commentary or judgment....Just be with the body and breath....Simply 'BE'....

Engage in this rather ordinary practice several times a day. It allows the thinking mind to rest, as your focus of attention is on the body and the breath.

Thought is a marvelous function of the mind but it also has the potential to create confusion, conflict, and wild imaginings.....The thought process can assemble unnecessary structures, that are not beneficial to you or the world you live in. Thought can and does, with the assistance of emotional energy, create a disastrous mess called "ME".

The body and breath practice presents the opportunity to step out of the relentless flow of thoughts. There is a gap, there is some space, but YOU are still there....awareness is still there.... and then you may notice that something is missing during this practice. Not just something, but THE thing. In that gap, there is no "ME"....

So can it be that simple? Is it possible to step out of "ME" just by turning our mind away from thought? Can we stay peacefully in the gap forever and ever? Well, we are after all thinking creatures. It's part of our nature, so thoughts will come again, even if you have created a large amount of space in your mind-stream. It is important to note that thought, by itself is not the problem. There is in all of us, until we dissolve it, an apparent thinker of the thoughts...someone is doing the thinking...Who is there?

It's "ME", of course, thinking the thoughts. "ME", which was created by thought has now taken over the thought process. The thoughts belong to "ME", that's what it tells you. I stated earlier that the body is not "ME", because "ME" will state that this body is mine, it belongs to "ME", which makes the body a possession of "ME". We have further evidence of this fact thanks to the exercise we engaged in. Awareness of the body and breath alone left "ME" behind....it wasn't there.... It is the same with thought. There is no thinker, no "ME" behind the thought. "ME" uses the body and mind to give it energy and substance. It will use anything and claim ownership of it to stay in charge....to stay alive.....

Your whole life has been run by "ME". It has a tremendous amount of momentum and the simple exercise you practiced, even if you practice it on a daily basis, is probably not enough to dissolve the very resilient "ME". The exercise may help a great deal, but leaving "ME" behind for good will take a mighty effort and great determination. So, we can intensify our efforts with several more tried and true practices.

The next practice is similar to the first, but requires more discipline and intensity of focus. If you are sitting in a chair, keep your feet on the ground....If you are sitting on the floor, cross your legs in front of you.....Keep your back straight, your eyes slightly open, and breathe through your nose....Put your tongue on the roof of your mouth, just behind your front teeth....Your hands will simply rest on your lap, hands up or down, your choice....

Now, simply observe your breath as it enters and exits your body.... You can focus on the air coming in and out of your nostrils, or on the rise and fall of your abdomen, or both......Observe the breath single pointedly....When thoughts arise, and they will, do not become distracted.....Just keep coming back to your breath if a thought has begun to pull you away....The same goes for any feelings and sense perceptions (sounds, etc.) that may arise....Stay focused on your breath....If you are distracted, come back to the breath....It is your anchor... The purpose of this practice is to develop a state of non-reaction and non-attachment to thoughts, feelings, and sense perceptions.....They are there at times, moving through you, but they are not you.....The activity of the mind will slow down and you will discover that the mind is essentially spacious and clear....You can become very peaceful during this practice. For some that will come quickly, for others it will take some time and effort. Be patient and persist. The disciplined mind, over time, will become less jumpy and more stable. It is not advisable to analyze the results of the practice...just do it. The goal is to calm the mind, to discover the quality of openness and formlessness that is always present, but never noticed. There will be opportunities for analysis and understanding during the more advanced practices that will follow. This calming practice is the foundation. We cannot behold the mind and understand its function if it is too busy and distracted by the myriad of forms that arise, abide, and dissolve continuously within it. The relentless activity of the mind left unchecked, will continuously assemble and erect structures, manufacture an endless variety of forms and concepts....Its crowning achievement is building the phantom called "ME".....Once the mind is calmer and you feel that the practice is bearing fruit, you can engage in the next technique.

In the next practice, which is sometimes called 'special insight', you will keep the same body position as the calming practice. They are similar in every way, except that the object of focus will be different; Instead of watching the breath, you will gently witness the activity of the mind itself. Thoughts, feelings, emotions, and sense perceptions are now the object of your awareness. You will simply observe them without attaching to them or elaborating on them. You will also not reject anything that arises in the mind....Just leave it as it is and be aware of the mind's activity.....

As you progress with the practice, ask yourself the following question; If you are watching your thoughts come and go, than can the thoughts be you? As you investigate deeply and persistently, you will see that they cannot. The same goes for feelings, emotions and sense perceptions. If the thoughts are not you, if they are just passing through the mind, then what they tell you about

41

who you are cannot be valid because you are the awareness observing them, and not the story they tell....The mind's content and movement are not you, they are foreign objects. Thoughts are not you and they don't belong to you, or to anyone. You are simply the awareness that is able to witness the mind's activity, and the more that this is realized, the more spacious and open you will feel.

You are awareness....clear and open....and so, as you contemplate this realization, ask yourself what has become of the ever present and all powerful "ME"? You will see directly that this concept, this lie, is just a thought pattern, energized by emotions. It's not you; you never were or will be "ME". It's merely an illusion that had created a state of delusion in your mind....

There is no "ME"....there never has been in reality. You were deceived by a thought, a concept, and the emotional energy associated with it. Your whole life has been a lie; your suffering and frustration have been unnecessary. "ME" was just a story that you believed to be true....a myth....Can you see it? Can you feel it?

There is no way to know for sure if the

development of "ME", this ego-centric perspective that plagues us, is a mistake, an aberration of some kind, or a natural part of the evolutionary process of humans, a stage of development that we are called on to engage and eventually transcend. What is clear, however, is that "ME" is problematic and is a disturbance to our peace of mind. It is also an obstacle that prevents us from living freely and creatively. "ME" must be eradicated, and the calming and insight practices can be a tremendously powerful antidote to the state of unconsciousness that the majority of human beings are immersed in. Practice on a daily basis if you can….

The practices do not have a set duration; for some, short sessions are better, for others, longer sessions may be more effective. What is more important than the length of time or the perfect technique, is the fervent desire to see the truth, to see what you really are….and aren't. If you are sincere and determined, you will have the best chance to overcome the phantom in your mind called "ME". It doesn't exist, and yet it will fight to the death to stay alive, to be in control…."ME" can die, but the real you cannot….

The real you is not a form, a thing....it is a formless awareness....Words will always fail to describe this awareness that you are because words are forms. You cannot think your way out of "ME", or debate your way out of it with deep philosophical ideas and concepts. Just be willing to look directly at your mind and see what is truly there. Is there an entity behind the scenes running the show, thinking the thoughts, feeling the feelings? If "ME" is real, you should be able to locate it upon investigation. Always remember, the YOU that is doing the investigating is not "ME". You, in this case, is the awareness and wisdom that is shining through the illusion of "ME"....

The following practice is the final one that you will need to engage in to bring "ME" into the light of awareness. The total dissolution of this 'ghost in the machine' may take time, so be patient....The light of awareness will weaken this imaginary structure, and bring increasing levels of clarity into your life. When "ME" is sufficiently weakened, it will fall away forever. This falling away can be dramatic, or simple and ordinary. It can happen in a variety of ways, but it must finally happen for the truth to be known, and for you to realize that you have never been a person, a "ME". You are far more, and yet, much less than you ever imagined yourself to be. Here is the final practice called self-inquiry....

There is no specific physical posture or position for this practice..... Begin by becoming completely aware of your sense impressions and your moving mind (thoughts and feelings)....You can then focus on any one of these with full attention....Let's use, for example, sight. Just see what is in front of you at that moment without commentary or judgment.....Then, ask yourself, "Who is seeing?"... Look within and locate the self, the "ME", or whatever may be there, that is having the experience of seeing....There is seeing happening....Is there anyone there having this experience? If you say to yourself, "Well, it's "ME" that is seeing", then locate where that "ME" resides....Is it in your eyes, your brain, your heart, your toes? Maybe it outside of your body altogether....Look there too.....Where is the "ME" that is seeing? You can use any of the sense modalities during this practice...."Who is thinking this thought?".... "Who is hearing this sound?"....And so on.....Is there an entity somewhere having this experience? Simply look within and without and see directly if a 'person' is there behind the scenes....See if "ME" is there at all....If you are unable to locate a solid, unchanging 'self' upon investigation, then you have discovered the non-existence of "ME"....And yet, there is an awareness that is present....A clear, still awareness.....That is who you are.....

Do this practice anytime...It is powerful!

Something is speaking to you....an inner voice, or feeling.....an intuition....your own innate wisdom. If this were not the case, you would never engage in the practices presented in this chapter. You would never have the courage or motivation to confront the imaginary monster that calls itself "ME".....

In a way, it is all very simplistic; a lack of awareness allows this apparition to develop and strengthen over time, supported by an environment of beings that are trapped in the same delusion. It feeds on thoughts and emotions when you are not paying attention. It grows and grows and runs your life.....But in reality, it isn't even there at all! Your mind is in a state of disorder and confusion due to a lack of conscious awareness, and "ME" exists, in appearance only, continuing to run the show while hiding in the shadows....

"ME" can dissolve slowly if you apply persistent clear awareness to your own mind's activity. As it weakens, you will notice a reduction of anxiety.... You will be grounded in the present moment....When it dissolves completely, you will be liberated forever from the illusory drama called "ME".

Is it possible to function in the world without a "ME", without a 'self'? It is worth finding out. The very idea of living a life without "ME" may seem strange and unimaginable. We are deeply habituated in a 'self' oriented point of reference; all of humanity shares this burden. It is a specific mode or style of consciousness that has become imbalanced, and upon this imbalance, we have erected a universe of dream figures and relationships that exist only in our minds....

"ME" is our own creativity and imagination gone

47

awry. To reclaim our sanity, we must have the courage to dissolve "ME" once and for all. It may be a major shock to the system when "ME" disappears and lives no more, but in reality, it will only be a shock to "ME". It wants to survive at all costs, and it may not die quietly. The awareness that you are, beyond form and identity, will remain as it always is; silent, peaceful, and clear.....

"ME"

"ME"

"ME"

"ME"

"ME"

"ME"

"ME"

© Beverlee Horowitz

5 CHAPTER – LIFE WITHOUT "ME"

A life without "ME" is simply life, the process of living, without the idea that there is someone behind the scenes that is living the life....

The world of phenomena in which the life process plays out is made up of the elements of earth (solidity), water (cohesion), fire (heat and light), air (movement), and space (the emptiness in which the other elements manifest). Every object in the universe is constructed from these elements. The objects themselves are the four elements moving and interacting in space. There is no solidity at all, in reality, and it is this fact that "ME" continually turned away from when it ran your life....

The universal intelligence and awareness that you are became obscured by a mental and emotional form that refused to change and flow amidst the dynamic energy that is the creative process. "ME" was a rejection of the natural process of movement and change. A rejection also of the intimate connection and interpenetration of all forms, which is the true nature of manifest phenomena. When your intelligence is obscured, there is the birth of ignorance, delusion. That obscuration, that delusion, is "ME"....

All forms, including what we call material, mental, and emotional, are temporary and fragile. Only the formless intelligence, the ever present awareness beyond form, is permanent and unchanging. When you are aware of this formless dimension, "ME" is nowhere to be found. When you realize you ARE this formless dimension, you are at home, and "ME" is a distant memory.....

When "ME" has dissolved considerably, or has disappeared altogether, you will realize yourself as space, awareness, and form simultaneously....You are space... You are no-thing, because you are essentially free of having any identity whatsoever. You are also form, both individually and collectively, as all forms are interdependent and cannot exist separately in reality; And of course, you are the awareness that knows this to be true....you are this intelligence...

Awareness is a mysterious formless knowing; it is the luminosity in the void, the emptiness which is the ground of all forms that arise. Awareness does not need an object, a 'something' to be aware of....it is aware of itself....it IS. It is untouched by the world of energy, movement, and formation, and yet, paradoxically, it is inseparable from the phenomenal world; it is the very ground of it. The formless and un-manifest luminous void is the source of all of the movement and formation that exists in the universe. You are this source, and when "ME" is no longer dominating your mind, you will realize this fact....

When the formless awareness becomes aware of an object, it can then be called a 'consciousness'. A consciousness is present when someone is aware of something. Here, we have a duality of subject and object, and there is a time and space element that is experienced by the mind. The apparent separation of the subject and object creates a sense of space because we become conscious of someone here, experiencing something over there. The mind creates this distinction. There is nothing that exists in reality that can be called 'space', since space is no-thing. It is the absence of form and not a thing in itself.....

We become aware of space, nothingness, when forms are manifested. Form and space, are a mutual perception....awareness of nothing and something arise simultaneously...

If I am 'here', and want to move to an object over 'there', I then create movement, which we experience as time. Our minds create it; it is not ultimately real, but it does exist as a conscious experience. So, the concept of time is our creation, as is the awareness of space, due to the presence of form. Space, form (energy), and awareness are inseparable….YOU are these three inseparable qualities….

The creation of "ME" prevented us from seeing and experiencing the subtle dimensions of our Being. "ME" is a consciousness attached to form, and this limited perspective creates suffering because it is out of sync with reality. There are no forms, really. There is only movement. Even this movement is not the ultimate truth. The formless dimension of space and awareness is the basis of all forms that arise, and it is the only permanent, unchanging truth. Energy and formation are relative truths that are never entirely true. A form may be true in the present moment, but it is changing continuously. This impermanence is the natural quality of phenomena, and for this reason, forms are not lasting, not ultimately true.

"ME" was simply a mental formation that became all encompassing, and the momentum of "ME" created a limitation that led to suffering and confusion. No "ME", no problem……This is the basis of life after "ME". Unlimited potential, creativity, and a pervasive sense of peacefulness become the focus of a life lived by no one. Can you see it? Can you feel it? You will be able to for sure when "ME" is seen as a non-existent phantom. You will even have a true taste of this state if "ME" has diminished sufficiently....

Life is a creative process, and it may be shocking at first to realize that there is no 'being' that is creating the universe....consciousness is the creator....it is no one, and belongs to no one. It is everything and nothing at once. "ME" wanted to be something forever. It was just a bad dream....for some, a nightmare....

As a form, we can understand ourselves using the example of a hurricane. The elements that constitute a hurricane are always present; when these elements interact based on certain causes and conditions, they take a noticeable formation. The National Weather Service will announce that we have a tropical wave present in the Atlantic or Pacific ocean. When the formation becomes more pronounced and definitive, and builds momentum, the tropical wave is then named.....Andrew, Katrina, etc.....We now have a tropical storm with a name; it has become an 'entity' in our mind. It maintains its entity status and name as it intensifies into a hurricane. The name and its status as an entity gives the hurricane an illusion of solidity. The radar, however, will show the movement of the storm over time, and it is obvious that there is continuous change within the structure of the storm....'Andrew' is not solid at all, it is changing constantly. Only the name and its status in our minds as an entity remains the same. As the storm becomes tighter and more contracted, its potential to destroy the environment increases; and yet, in the center of this destructive force of nature, is an empty center, called the 'eye'. It is still and peaceful in the center of this raging elemental form. The storm will rage on until it interacts with land. This will alter its structure, and the 'entity' will begin to disintegrate until it no longer has a name, or a definable formation. So what happened to the elements that comprised this storm? Nothing.....they are still present, as they were before the storm's formation, and during its journey as a named entity. Nothing has changed except the particular form that the storm had become. The form lives no more, but the truth is, that the form was never stable or the same for a moment. It was always changing and had no essential nature, and yet, we perceived it as a manifestation with solidity and continuity over time. This was never true....just look closely. Entities, like the hurricane, have no essence and no sustainability. You, as a form, are the same as the hurricane. Can you see it? Can you feel it?

"ME" was the refusal to see the truth of non-self, non-solidity. "ME" was just a concept that was unable and unwilling to see the truth. All forms are empty of an identity....empty of solidity....empty of permanence and continuity. You, as a form, are simply an interplay of the elements, that are moving, shifting, and changing unceasingly. There is not and never was anything to grasp onto that has stability and duration. You, as a form, are movement, change....What makes you different than the hurricane is that you can know this directly. The awareness, the intelligence that you essentially are, is formless, permanent, and unchanging.... it is your true nature....

"ME" was a veil obscuring this truth. Now, you know this directly. If there is still some measure of fear that arises as you contemplate this reality, it is simply "ME" trying to hold on to its illusory existence. Give it a kiss and say goodbye. Be loving as you send it away forever, or rather, as you see it for the mirage that it is. "ME" does not know how to love because its nature is exclusively to manifest as a state of fear and paranoia. Just love it to death, with clear awareness and compassion, and let life express itself through the awareness that you are…..

Find the still, clear space, at the center of your personal storm called "ME"….

The eye of your storm is free of anger, anxiety, fear, attachment, and ignorance….Know it….Be it….

The world of manifest forms, of energy and movement, is not external to us, or for that matter, internal. External and internal are merely reflections of each other, so it is not necessary to put phenomena into categories. The 'moving mind', which is consciousness individually and collectively, is both the creator and the creation.

The content of your 'moving mind' shapes your vision, your world, and since all phenomena and all minds are connected and interdependent, the collective 'moving mind' is a co-creator that greatly influences your individual consciousness. This 'moving mind' is the totality of all manifested forms. This, and any other possible universe, is just consciousness itself...it is the creator and destroyer....

The tendency of the mind to grasp form and erect concepts is what led to the construction of an entity that has no real existence. This is how "ME" developed over time. Building this entity that you believed was the real you, gives rise to the tendency to perceive entities everywhere. The world of movement becomes a world of separate beings, and all of the 'entities' compete to be in power. Some of these entities may seem like they are part of you; that they come from within. Others may feel alien, like an unwanted external manifestation that you are confronted with. In either case, they just ARE. The categories of inner and outer will not assist you toward clarity. Entities will appear to your consciousness as a solid self-sustaining form if you are in a state of unawareness, but they are, in reality, fluid....they are not solid and unchanging.....

When "ME" has dissolved completely or has weakened to a great degree, the tendency to see inherently existing entities will diminish, and eventually cease. All forms are like the hurricane, and you will realize that they are moving, flowing and shifting, and that there is no essential nature to be found. Entities appear to exist, but ultimately do not….this is the true nature of form….of you as a form…….

The phenomenal world does not have to be problematic, does not have to be conflicted. It will express itself through you joyfully when "ME" is no more.

The world of movement and formation IS consciousness. There are no 'beings' that are conscious, the world is just the cosmic dream playing itself out in an infinity of forms, and in a variety of dimensions. It is possible to be an active co-creator in your world and it becomes natural and workable when "ME" is not running the show. This does not mean that you will necessarily have every selfish desire and whim fulfilled; it is more a state in which personal compulsive desires are reduced and no longer dictate your thoughts, feelings and activities. It is realizing a state of 'being' that at once lives out its desires, and yet is completely beyond them, as the ever- present 'Witness'. This paradox at first may seem to be an impossibility to actualize, but when "ME" is seen as a mere creation in your mind, you will realize yourself being formless in essence (emptiness/space) and nature (awareness), and yet, as a form as well. These three dimensions are inseparable; they are unified. You are nothing, everything, and a particular thing all at once. Knowing the truth beyond the limited perception of "ME" is freedom….liberation…… It is possible, or even likely, that you will begin to lose interest in many of the ideas and activities that once motivated you once "ME" is a distant memory. The quality of being 'driven' to engage in certain endeavors will decrease or disappear altogether. Without the 'driven' quality, which is a form of personal attachment , it is still possible, however, to engage in activities that you enjoyed in the past without having them define you. With "ME" out of the picture, there is nothing to prove, and you will no longer seek to build your identity based on what you do, say, or think. You can now, if you choose to, enjoy creating freely and naturally with no agenda that is tied to a self-image….

Radically free and totally present….Unencumbered by

"ME".....

Lila is a Sanskrit word that is often translated as 'play' or 'play of the Gods'. There are an infinity of possible creative expressions, and the world of phenomena is ready and open to be played with. There was very little, or no possibility for "ME" to create joyfully and freely. "ME" was concerned with trying to manipulate the world to find security at all costs. Engaging in a stressful endeavor such as this left "ME" with no options, no space to 'play' in the world of form. Attempting to secure yourself in a continuous tidal wave of change is very serious business. 'Lila' is not compatible with seriousness, tension, stress, and fear....

Will there be exclusively the experience of 'oneness' after "ME" has faded away? Will the 'one' stand alone? If so, then why did the Enlightened Masters of the past 2,500 years teach beings how to wake up from the dream of independent selfhood? If there is only 'oneness', then who were they interacting with? If you realize 'oneness' after life as "ME", is there anyone else existing in the world besides you? This concept is often misunderstood, but it will become clear once life without "ME" becomes more familiar and natural....

There is one essence, and one nature (emptiness/awareness). In moving mind consciousness, however, there is always duality, as the experience of being a conscious subject is inseparable from the appearance of an object being perceived. Subject and object appear to be separate, but they are, in reality, completely interdependent....separate in appearance, but essentially 'one'. Realizing the truth of this paradox allows for the 'play' of the manifest world to express itself without conflict. Opposites do not have to be in opposition to each other, they are co-creators in the world of energy/form. "ME" was a paranoid subjective manifestation that felt truly separate from its environment....it was a toxic ingredient in the cosmic soup....

So, is there 'oneness' or not? Well, YOU are actually nothing, everything, and a particular thing all at once. Emptiness/awareness is formless, no-thing.... you are that; so, in essence and nature, you are nothing'. As a form, however, you are an individual, so you are also a 'particular' expression of consciousness; and, since all forms are interdependent energetic expressions and have no true separate existence, you are also 'everything', the totality of consciousness. When "ME" was in charge, there was a lack of knowledge of this essential truth, because "ME" was an energetic contraction that focused solely on itself. "ME" was a state of self-absorption that refused to look beyond its narrow self-imposed boundaries, because it was merely a state of fear in a hazy dream....

Individuality and personality are often understood as two words that describe the same phenomena; they are, however, quite different. You, as an individual, are a particular expression of consciousness with your own point of reference. You are a specific, unique portal of the conscious experience. This does not mean that you are permanent and unchanging. The individual is the "I", the sense of self, that is momentary....it is intermittent. Because it is changing moment to moment, we can say that the individual is discontinuous.

It is a phenomena that flashes in and out of existence incessantly. The "I" is also, however, continuous because each moment of existence conditions the next, and so on, and so on. So, there is a continuous discontinuity that we call "I", the individual. It is a valid consciousness despite being illusory....it is and it isn't, and that is consistent with the ultimate truth of space (non-existence), and awareness (existence). The individual is conventionally real, but not ultimately real....

Personality is "ME", a figment of the imagination with no validity, no existence even conventionally. There are no 'persons' in the world, only stories that take shape over time, conditioned by an external environment that is equally unreal....it is completely mind created....made up....many masks for many occasions....a dream that is fading away.....fading fast.....

"I" is and isn't......"ME" never was......

The world of energy/form has limitless possibilities of manifestation; a variety of dimensions that differ qualitatively. Many spiritual traditions refer to hierarchies or levels of evolution to describe how the realms of spirit and form co-exist. Mystical experiences are possible for spiritual seekers as they engage in their vision quest, and many of these events are illuminating, and inspiring. The seeker may realize that they and the world that they are familiar with do not exist in a limited, predictable fashion. There are so many realms, so many experiences to engage in, amazing for sure, and yet, a mind that continually seeks experiences can become attached to the spiritual smorgasbord that it encounters, and find itself further distracted and entertained. It is possible in these circumstances for "ME" to slip in through the back door and reassert itself....

Be watchful...."ME" cannot survive in the light of awareness...Let life live you....A life of truth, peace, and clarity......

6 CHAPTER – SOCIETY WITHOUT "ME"

Many people have a cynical attitude regarding the possibility of improving society and creating a peaceful, cooperative environment that emphasizes love, creativity, and non-aggression. Some will mock this notion and claim that a utopian society is a fantasy, a wild imagining. An idea that is impossible to realize, and yet, not only do we imagine a society that emphasizes selfish desires, a lust for power, and a tendency toward aggression and violence, we have actually managed to create and live in such a society. We have imagined and actualized a dysfunctional society, but for some reason, we find it impossible to imagine and actualize a society based on reason and harmony. The reason for this limited vision of human potential is "ME" and "WE". A society based on a selfish, disconnected mind-set cannot envision a naturally interdependent society that functions as an organism oriented toward growth, knowledge, and truth....

Let us now begin to imagine a society free of "ME" and "WE"....let's create a masterpiece, free of delusion.

But first, before creating a vision of a sane, functional society, it is important to understand what went wrong in a society that is primarily insane and dysfunctional. I will use the current United States of America as an example of a dysfunctional society. Most societies on the planet are probably similar since "ME" and "WE" are the driving force for humans at this time, but I will focus on society in the USA since I know it directly....

First of all, there is an obvious class system in the USA, which creates disharmony and fuels feelings of superiority, inferiority, envy, and apathy. Our species has played this game of the 'haves' and 'have not's' in one way or another for as long as we have had recorded history, but right now, the society in the Unites States has created an extreme version of class disparity that is creating discord and despair for the majority of its citizens. The development of such a lopsided class system is closely tied to the control of resources, and manipulation of the financial system. There is clearly a "WE" in the upper class that wants to remain in power....in control......

Once there is a "WE" in control of a society, many other "WE's" will emerge. Some will work alongside of the controlling "WE" and try to get a VIP pass to the upper levels. Others will consider themselves victims in a game that is rigged against them. In the USA, the categories of rich, upper middle class, middle class, lower middle class, and the poor have solidified the citizens into a static mode of existence, with the false appearance of upward mobility firmly established. This tactic keeps the bottom dwellers in their place. They are fed hope, but the situation has become hopeless.....

The ruling class is able to keep the game going endlessly by using the news and entertainment media, which they own, to further condition the masses. This creates a society of fearful robots who dare not question the activities of those in authority, and so the game goes on. It goes on because people want to believe in something, they want to feel secure. All of the little frightened "ME's", and the puny "WE's" that are assembled from them, do not even dream that they are in reality, powerful, creative beings. They have been blinded by the conditioning from above to believe in a government that does not have their best interests at heart. They have been fooled by a financial system that is completely controlled, and driven by profit margins. This corrupt capitalistic distortion places the bottom line above the welfare of the beings in the society. Profit is the primary goal because it makes the "WE" at the top bigger, stronger, and more powerful. Every "ME" and "WE" wants to continue....wants to grow....that is always the ultimate goal....

So what has society in the good ole US of A accomplished? What has "WE" managed to create, led by its governing bodies, and financial institutions? The answer is obvious: Wars, poverty, high rates of murders and other crimes, depression, eating disorders, mental and emotional illness, a deficient education system....the list could go on and on. Have you had enough? Is this the best that the citizens of this country can do? As long as "ME" and "WE" are in charge, then yes, this is the best that all of us can do....

The basis of a sane society is a sane individual. A degenerate society, like the USA and so many others on this planet, cannot be improved by violent overthrow, or even by peacefully marching in the street. Each citizen must take responsibility for their own awakening out of the nightmare of "ME". When there are enough aware and sane individuals in a society, the changes that are required will happen naturally and peacefully.....
Remember, there is no all-powerful "WE" without all of the "ME's" that energize it. Every individual

that dissolves the grand delusion of "ME" can easily influence others to do the same. Some will run away and seek shelter in the status quo, but others will listen and eventually seek the truth. All that is required are enough individuals that want to stop suffering, enough that want to be sane. A new world awaits us.....

The individuals in power and their corporations have complete control of the distribution of the natural resources that give us the energy that we all require to live a high quality life. The idea that anyone can own land, oil, precious minerals, and even water, is a notion that is at once absurd, and also very dangerous. The very idea of 'ownership' is a fundamental concept that fuels the existence and power structure of "ME" and "WE".....

So, the first thing that is required in a sane society is the eradication of the concept of ownership. Isn't it strange that we have accepted the idea that someone can own a piece of land, or even the water that flows on it? What right does anyone have to make such a claim? The concept of ownership is based on selfish desire and an inclination toward gaining power over others who own less or nothing. It's "ME" and "WE" doing what they do; attempting to get bigger and stronger and trying to continue at all costs....

A sane society will manage the equitable distribution of resources so that all beings on the planet can eat, drink, breathe, and have access to energy that will give them all of the options needed to live life to the fullest. Everyone is aware of the alternative energy sources that will replace fossil fuels. It is a matter of maximizing these potential sources of energy and allowing for all beings on the planet to benefit from having access to clean, free energy.....yes, FREE. If no one owns the natural resources on our planet, then there is no cost involved in benefitting from what nature has made available. The twisted logic of "ME" and "WE" is deeply ingrained in our minds, and it is time for all of us to be brave enough to make a radical shift in our thinking. The shift is simply to view the Earth and its resources as belonging equally to everyone. What a shame that such an obvious and basic concept has to be viewed as a radical shift, but "ME" and "WE" have done a number on us all. Human beings have accepted an insane view of reality, of life, and the result has been a society of class warfare, violence, and manipulation....enough is enough! Ownership will be a thing of the past in a sane society...

It is not even necessary to own items that you want to enjoy for a hobby, or for temporary enjoyment. How many people have a boat sitting on their driveway that they use infrequently or never? How many have musical instruments collecting dust in the corner of the room that haven't been played in years? Is it necessary to 'own' these items? It is for "ME" because "ME" is all about possessions, and the value of these possessions for "ME" is that they are able to be added to their story....the story of "ME". However, if "ME" is not dominating a society, then people can use what they need, when they need it, and then share it with others when they no longer have a use for it. A sane society may even develop 'rental' sites that house specialty items that can be borrowed for as long as they are needed, and then returned so that others may use them. If you are using an item for a lifetime, then keep it. If not, then why hold on to it? Material items are meant to be used and enjoyed, not held on to for the purpose of proving your worth. There are so many possibilities that will become apparent when "ME" and "WE" are seen as mere illusions...

Now let's go even further. With the concept of

ownership no longer relevant, let us now imagine a society without money. Yes, I have stated the unthinkable! No money? How will we purchase what we need to survive? Even more importantly, what will motivate us to DO anything?

First, let's examine closely what the monetary system has given us; what it has contributed to society. Yes, money is used as an exchange to receive products and services, but does everyone have equal access to money? No....Our monetary system and all of the financial institutions that control the money flow and interest rates, are not concerned with the equal distribution of the paper or digital images on a screen that they ascribe a particular value to. We have a system that is rigged to favor those in power, and we have accepted a hierarchy that dictates who makes more money than others. Bankers, lawyers, and CEO's of corporations, for example, make more than teachers or factory workers. Why? It's just the way it is, according to those in charge who have conditioned us to accept this structural distortion as a fact of life, a natural occurrence. Those in control of the monetary system use it to control the masses, and this manipulation has become a major factor in the development of the current 'class system' that creates a society of inequality and discord.....

The argument that the need to make money is the driving force that motivates us to do what we do is weak and ultimately inaccurate. Isn't it possible to have a society of individuals that engage in the activities that they enjoy for the sake of enjoyment? Does a person with a special talent need a reason to actively engage their gift? Of course not....The need to make money has created the motivation for most citizens to become wage slaves, and more often than not, they are not performing tasks that they enjoy, or that feature their unique talents....

A society can exist and flourish as a community of individuals that have a shared responsibility for meeting everyone's needs. Those with talents can use those talents for their own fulfillment, and also as a contribution to the society at large. As long as the necessary resources are available, there would be no problem with the society functioning interdependently. An individual with a talent as a technician can contribute to the technological advances of the society. Healers will heal, entertainers will entertain, artists will create, farmers will farm, and so on....

Goodbye bankers, lawyers, stockbrokers, and any profession that had finances as its core function or value. With the class system dissolved, there are no longer the rich and the poor, so the motivation for criminal activity would decrease greatly, or disappear all- together. So, goodbye police officers, parole officers, and of course, goodbye military!

The possibilities are endless in a sane society free of "ME" and "WE", and probably unimaginable to many at this point in time, but it will be a reality when "ME" no longer dominates. A sane society would not be perfect, not a 'utopia', but it would be an environment of cooperation that promotes freedom and equality, and that would be reward enough. Human beings are capable of awakening from the dream of "ME"....it starts with you.....

You are a powerful Being.....A Creator....

Fully realize your unlimited potential....*Create Heaven here and NOW...*

7 CHAPTER - RELATIONSHIPS WITHOUT "ME"

Our life is an infinite series of relationships,

from the smallest levels of microcosm, to the largest levels of macrocosm. There are truly no independent existences. Interdependence is the fundamental basis of all manifested phenomena, of all energetic movement and formations….

There is continuous cooperation between a large variety of systems that function together to allow for life, as we know it, to exist. Nothing exists on its' own; nothing is separate and autonomous. Relationship is always and everywhere the truth of existence. It is the very ground of creation.

From the subatomic levels, to the atomic, to the molecular, to the cellular, to the organic, and on and on, and on….all is relationship, and all of this is LOVE….Love wants nothing for itself, because it is always and only connection and cooperation, and the very idea of separation is impossible to fathom when love expresses itself as the creative process. All of creation on all levels is love, even if there is no awareness or acknowledgement of this basic fact. We, as organic beings residing on an object floating in space that we call Earth, are on a mission to discover how we are connected to everything in the Cosmos. We are on a mission to discover all of the relationships to all of the beings that cooperate to create this experience we call humanity. We are on a mission to discover love; to become aware that everything is love. We discover this truth by understanding relationship on all levels, with full appreciation and reverence. This is our mission, and only one thing stands in the way, if we allow it to.... that thing is "ME"....

We have seen throughout the course of this book how this contraction of mental and emotional energy called "ME" creates dissatisfaction and discontent for individuals, for societies, and for the world at large. If we look closely, we can see that "ME" is creating disturbances to relationships on every scale. Healthy, thriving relationships, and "ME" cannot co-exist....

There are certain primary relationships that shape the lives of human beings. Parent and child relationships, sibling relationships, extended family relationships, romantic relationships, and close friendships are all connections that have a major influence on our quality of life. These relationships can be supportive and uplifting, or a drain on our energy. The key factor that determines the quality of these relationships is the degree of "ME" that is involved in these interactions.

First, let's explore the parent/child relationship. It is often said that a parent, and a mother in particular, have unconditional love for their child. This may be true in some cases, but is not necessarily true across the board. Parents are a product of their environment, and most, to be honest, have "ME" running their lives, and strongly influencing how they will interact with and raise their child. There are always varying degrees of "ME", depending on the particular parent's upbringing and genetic make-up. A very small number of parents may be free of "ME" completely....

A relatively small number may be free of this self-absorbed state of mind to a large degree, but this is far from the norm. The truth is, many parents are heavily influenced by "ME", and some may even be completely controlled by their conditioning and exist totally in the grasp of "ME". The degree of "ME" present in the parent will determine how 'unconditional ' the love for their child truly is. It will also determine to what degree the child will be taught to be a "ME", as a parent's influence tends to be the strongest element of all in shaping a child's future behavior and outlook.

So, we often see parent and child relationships that involve power struggles, as the parent's vision of the future for their child is not in accord with the child's inclinations. The parent may appear to be justified in wanting what is 'best' for their child, but when "ME" is involved, the parent is often seeking to control the child's future, so they can be free of worry and feel a sense of peace. It is essentially a self-serving attitude. This is very common, and because it is so widespread, it appears to be 'normal'. It is, in fact, the norm because most parents behave this way to some degree or other. The norm, however, is not necessarily the best we can do. Dysfunctional relationships are often the norm, but no one would defend them as appropriate just because they are prevalent....

So we have "ME", more often than not, raising a child to be a "ME", and there is little room for true communication because both sides are too busy defending their mental positions; they are both protecting their territory. Is love present in a "ME" driven parent/child relationship? True love is always there, attempting to shine through the thick wall of self-absorption. It will shine brighter as "ME" diminishes, and manifest fully when the delusion of separate selfhood vanishes. A parent and child can then enjoy a loving relationship that is not based on selfish attachment and expectations….they will be free to love….they will serve the relationship, and not expect to be served by it. "ME" will vanish and love will remain…

Attachment serves "ME"…Love always seeks to serve the other…Attachment is a manifestation of fear and confusion….

Love is the essence of all relationship without "ME"…..

There are two important aspects that will be fully realized in any relationship that is largely or completely free of "ME". These are, the experience of spaciousness and the experience of 'nowness'. Our essence is space, non-existence. When we are aware of this truth, the spacious quality of our true nature is able to be experienced, felt, in the ever-changing realm of illusory form. Relationship is the basis of this realm of form, which means that relationship is ultimately unreal. It does, however, exist as the foundation of the cosmic dream; the conventional reality....

The truth behind relationship, then, is the paradox of nothing masquerading as an infinite number of something's. These something's relate to each other, and the realm of energy/form then manifests like a mirage in the desert. The more that a sense of space is realized in a relationship, the truer it will be, and the less problematic....

You are Space...And the Love that fills it...

The aspect of 'nowness', the present moment, is where relationship takes place. It is the meeting of two energetic forces that gives birth to a third force, which is the relationship. This all takes place in the timeless present moment. The past is memory, which is merely a mental image, and the future is only our imagination, fueled by expectations and hope. There is no relationship in the past or future since they are only in the mind of the subject. They are mental wanderings, dreams that are not real even conventionally. The past and future are subjective 'imaginings' that are based on the conventional reality, but they are far less real.

84

Conventional reality is the present moment....it is relationship and interdependence....We can call it a 'real dream' even though it is ultimately unreal, because it is the highest truth in the realm of form, the dimension of manifest phenomena.

The truth of nothing and everything is 'now'....

Every relationship that is imbued with a sense of spaciousness, and is grounded in the present moment, expresses the highest truth that can be conveyed in the dimension of energy/form. It is the nature of the Cosmos on all scales to be in relationship. It is actually more accurate to say that the Cosmos IS relationship. Is it possible for us human beings, as we are presently conditioned, to bring the natural truth of space and presence into our relationships, as we define them? It is possible for sure, but not an easy task, especially when "ME" is in the picture. "ME" forever attempts to fill the space out of fear of non-existence, and also dwells exclusively in the past and future. "ME" is only a story, and all stories feed off of past memories and project a future outcome. This is why "ME" finds it impossible to truly relate....it is never here and now, where all relationship takes place. So, how can we bring spaciousness and 'nowness' to our relationships, and lessen the influence of this paranoid clot of attention, called "ME"? Let us now investigate this process, as it relates to the complex world of romantic relationships...

Romantic relationships are what most people are referring to when they use the word relationship. They are very important to the majority of human beings, and often give a sense of completion and connection that cannot be found elsewhere. Romantic love is intense and can be overwhelming, due to the strong chemical reactions elicited by the flow of sexual energy when it is fully activated. When "ME" is under the spell of 'Eros', the lovers are usually in for a ride that includes the high of blissful union, and the low that often manifests as longing, possessiveness, and jealously. This kind of ride is both exciting and painful, and never fully satisfying. It is a dysfunctional roller coaster ride made possible by expectations for a future outcome. As always, "ME" is seeking reassurance and trying desperately to hold on to the blissful experiences. This approach will surely trigger a sense of frustration because the bliss is fleeting, and impossible to possess. When this is realized, feelings of longing, and the fear that you will lose the bliss forever, manifest as an emotional disturbance....pleasure has transformed into suffering...

Despite the suffering, human beings pursue romantic love relationships frequently and intensely. They become easily addicted to the chemical reactions created by the sexual energy flow, and this tends to make the lovers irrational, and keeps them in a state of anxiety until their next 'fix'. But, that is only half the problem...."ME", as always, seeks security....

So, the romantic couple will now attempt to secure a guarantee that the relationship will continue. What often follows are promises and vows such as, 'I am yours and you are mine, forever', or the ever popular, 'till death do us part'. The problem is that the participants cannot, in all likelihood, keep the promise since the individual at point 'A' is not identical to the individual at point 'B'. Time has passed, and since the individuals do not exist as solid, permanent, unchanging entities, the person who made the vow no longer exists down the road. Change has been the only constant, so the search for security is itself a state of suffering. It creates unnecessary anxiety, but despite this, the romantic partners will routinely claim each other as a possession to have and to hold....'My husband', 'my wife', 'my girlfriend', 'my boyfriend'....As usual, "ME" is doing its thing.

The result is, more often than not, romantic relationships that do not last, or that exist primarily in a state of dysfunction. In this day and age, couples who are not happy together will separate much more quickly than in years past. The social norms have changed, and couples no longer have to pretend that they are happy and fulfilled when they are not. It is no longer shameful to have a marriage fail, and this makes it possible for the individuals to be honest and to move on when they have 'changed' or have grown out of the relationship...Despite this, "ME", still dreams of a predictable and safe future, but there is no such thing!

Romantic relationships between individuals that are mostly or completely free of "ME" will have a very different dynamic. There will be no promises or vows since these are based on wishful thinking and future expectations. Romantic relationships free of "ME" have only one rule….they must exist in the

Here & Now…

We are very conditioned to think about relationships in terms of memories (the past), or projections based on a wish, and supported by vows or promises (the future). If "ME" is no longer a dominating force in the relationship, it will have a very different appearance. It will not necessarily even look like a relationship on the surface. Relationships in general are the coming together of two energies that create a third force as they merge together….

A kiss is a relationship! A beautiful moment when two individuals come together to create a third energy, which is the energy of passion….It is real and true, and fleeting. It cannot be captured or possessed….

Relationship is always about joining and releasing. Without "ME", the moment is released, and at the same time, it is cherished, but there is no expectation to have it occur again, and no paranoid grasping at possible future events. The beauty of the relationship, the kiss in this instance, will linger, and perhaps lead naturally to another moment...

When enough moments are strung together out of the natural momentum created by the passion, there appears to be a long-term relationship between the individuals. What is real, however, is that there is a series of moments appearing to be continuous. Each moment is unique and IS relationship. A twenty year long string of moments is no different than a five month long string of moments, if they are qualitatively the same. The string can be broken at any time, for a multitude of reasons, but the quality of those moments, those relationships, are eternal...they take their place in eternity as we let them go. Nothing can be held onto for the simple reason that there is no one existing as a solid, continuous being to begin with. The acceptance of change and movement is the acceptance of reality. In each moment, you are perfect as you are. You essentially are relationships existing on many levels. There is no YOU outside of relationship, outside of interdependence. When two forces meet, a third is created...it is momentary and it is beautiful...it does not need to be possessed to be of value. In fact, trying to possess it will surely destroy its' beauty....

A kiss Is a moment of Heaven.....

To be cherished

& released....

Honor it, and it will honor you...

Anyone functioning primarily as "ME", will likely see the ideas just expressed as out of sync with reality, or as an excuse to be a 'free spirit' and avoid commitment. Ironically, we are already 'free spirits'....that is our true nature....We are, in truth, free and unobstructed. We, however, often choose construct the chains that bind us. These chains are formulated out of the mental positions, the concepts, that we hold to be true....these chains are the building blocks of "ME"....

Relationship is sacred and impossible to grasp. True love is always available if we unclench our fists, unfold our arms, and open them wide to embrace the universe as an interdependent whole. Romantic love can be a challenging arena, and will surely be problematic to some degree if the participants are invested in their false identity.

91

When we approach romantic love in the moment, without expectations, we approach the bliss of union, unfettered by selfish desire. If we are open, the world will fill us. This is love without a goal....without a self....without "ME"......

However it is that we categorize the relationships in our lives, in all of them there is an intrinsic beauty and harmony. When we are present, clear, and peaceful, it is possible to tune into the natural, radiant quality that all relationships display. If we are instead in a state of mind that builds concepts and creates judgments, then the relationships in our lives will vary in quality, and will often become problems instead of blessings. Relationships free of "ME" are the very foundation of the world of form, and are always moving, always changing, and that, in itself, is beauty and truth....

Parent, child, lover, friend....these are labels that we use to describe the ever flowing, momentary connections that make the process of living possible. If we use the labels as a convenience and a tool of communication, then they are useful and practical as we navigate the world of energy/form. It is only when these labels become solidified concepts in our minds that they become limitations that cultivate ignorance, which is the root of the suffering mind...the mind of "ME"....

Suffering is only real

to "ME".....

"ME" is not real, so

suffering is not real...

Know this & you are free.......

A clear individual fully realizes that relationship is the basis of an atom, a molecule, a cell, an organism, a community, a society, a nation, a planet, a sun/star, a solar system, a galaxy, a universe, a multiverse, and on, and on, and on......Relationship is the truth of phenomena on all levels, in all dimensions. The 'moving mind', which is consciousness, IS relationship. It exists interdependently, it does not exist on its own. You do not exist on your own. Belief in an autonomous 'self', is the foundation of "ME", and it is a lie....a delusion...

As we take the time and make the effort to quiet the mind, to be with our breath, to witness the mind and its movement, and to become fully aware that we are awareness itself, let us realize that we are engaging in the process of knowing ourselves beyond name and form. This journey ends where it began....in clear, luminous space. The journey is not real....Nothing is real, and in this we find our peace. We find the truth that we have always been....

Pacing anxiously in the room you call life, and seeing a door with a silent knock from the other side....But if you open it, you must leave the room, and enter another, with different furniture...Maybe ugly, perhaps beautiful, or a bit of both... But new and scary, like looking in the mirror and seeing another face...Not yours, but a new mask, from the new room; With yet another door that may lead out of the castle altogether….To a bonfire of masks, rooms, and dreams….

Final Thoughts

It is a common assumption that human beings are radically free to make choices that will shape their lives. The journey toward dissolving the illusion of "ME" can begin simply by investigating how much free will you actually have.

Are you in control of your emotions? Are you reacting to circumstances without being fully aware of your thoughts, feelings, and emotions? Can you break habits that are well established, simply by making the choice to do so? The realization that you behave primarily as a machine programmed by external and internal events is a major step toward liberation….freedom. There is nothing that you have to believe in order to be free. The realization that you are not free will be the catalyst for change; a change from limitation and unconsciousness, to a realization of the amazing conscious Being that you are....

Just look within and see for yourself...Beyond the lie of "ME", you can exercise the only choice that really matters....And choose love over fear.....

Made in the USA
San Bernardino, CA
15 June 2015